CELEBRATING THE CITY OF SAINT PETERSBURG

Celebrating the City of Saint Petersburg

Walter the Educator

Silent King Books

SILENT KING BOOKS

SKB

Copyright © 2024 by Walter the Educator

All rights reserved. No part of this book may be reproduced in any manner whatsoever without written permission except in the case of brief quotations embodied in critical articles and reviews.

First Printing, 2024

Disclaimer
This book is a literary work; the story is not about specific persons, locations, situations, and/or circumstances unless mentioned in a historical context. Any resemblance to real persons, locations, situations, and/or circumstances is coincidental. This book is for entertainment and informational purposes only. The author and publisher offer this information without warranties expressed or implied. No matter the grounds, neither the author nor the publisher will be accountable for any losses, injuries, or other damages caused by the reader's use of this book. The use of this book acknowledges an understanding and acceptance of this disclaimer.

Celebrating the City of Saint Petersburg is a little collectible souvenir book that belongs to the Celebrating Cities Book Series by Walter the Educator. Collect them all and more books at WaltertheEducator.com

USE THE EXTRA SPACE TO TAKE NOTES AND DOCUMENT YOUR MEMORIES

SAINT PETERSBURG

In the northern reaches where the Neva flows,

Celebrating the City of Saint Petersburg

A city gleams with palatial prose.

Saint Petersburg, where history weaves,

A tapestry that never leaves.

From Peter's dream to modern grace,

A city born in regal place.

Bridges span like outstretched arms,

Connecting hearts, igniting charms.

The Winter Palace, an opulent sight,

Glistening beneath the polar night.

Echoes of Czars within its walls,

Silent whispers, grandiose halls.

White Nights blanket with endless light,

Celebrating the City of Saint Petersburg

Where dawn and dusk entwine in flight.

The Hermitage with treasures rare,

Art and culture, beyond compare.

Cobbled streets that tell a tale,

Of revolution, winds that wail.

Auroras dance on Baltic shores,

Mysteries of the past implore.

Nevsky Prospekt, a bustling vein,

Celebrating the City of
Saint Petersburg

Where past and present intertwine, remain.

Trams and whispers, old and new,

Stories in every brick accrue.

The Bronze Horseman, sentinel true,

Guardian of dreams that grew.

Petersburg's pulse, in metal cast,

Bridging future, echoing past.

Canals like veins through city spread,

Reflecting skies of blue and red.

Catherdral's domes in golden hue,

Rise to heavens, a celestial view.

Summer Gardens, verdant peace,

Where every care can find release.

Marble statues, flora bright,

An Eden in the urban might.

The Neva's banks, where poets tread,

With quills that bled, and verses read.

Pushkin's voice and Dostoevsky's pen,

Immortalize the souls of men.

A phoenix risen from marsh and mire,

Built on dreams, and fierce desire.

Imperial past and future bright,

Saint Petersburg, a beacon of light.

Celebrating the City of
Saint Petersburg

ABOUT THE CREATOR

Walter the Educator is one of the pseudonyms for Walter Anderson. Formally educated in Chemistry, Business, and Education, he is an educator, an author, a diverse entrepreneur, and he is the son of a disabled war veteran. "Walter the Educator" shares his time between educating and creating. He holds interests and owns several creative projects that entertain, enlighten, enhance, and educate, hoping to inspire and motivate you. Follow, find new works, and stay up to date with
Walter the Educator™ at
WaltertheEducator.com.

www.ingramcontent.com/pod-product-compliance
Lightning Source LLC
LaVergne TN
LVHW012048070526
838201LV00082B/3860